HOW TO APPEAR PERFECTLY INDIFFERENT WHILE CRYING ON THE INSIDE

JAY WINSTON RITCHIE

Metatron
Montréal

Second Edition
First printing

Layout and editing | Ashley Opheim
Cover art | Claire Milbrath

Metatron Press
5555 Avenue de Gaspe, Studio 305
Montréal, Quebec
H2T 2A3

ISBN 978-0-9936174-0-9

Contents

How to Appear Perfectly Indifferent While Crying on the Inside

I WANT TO DIE IN A HORRIBLE PLANE CRASH IN REMOTE EAST AFRICA

I want to die in a horrible plane crash in remote
   East Africa.
I want a lioness to consume my body and nap in
   the sun.

I want a Nairobi poacher to capture the lioness and
   sell her to the San Diego Zoo for 75,000 USD.

I want the lioness to experience a throbbing
   nostalgia for remote East Africa for the rest of
   her captive life
but be unable to articulate that throbbing nostalgia
   to her new peer group for fear of misrepresenting
   a fundamental part of her "self"—

not that the micro-culture fostered by the exhibit
   would understand—

the enclosure being full of "party lions",
their extrovert tendencies only accentuating her
   introversion,

the lioness incapable of vocalizing anything on the
   subject other than a forlorn, self-pitying, whiny
   moan uttered when in relative solitude.
I want this to be my afterlife.
I want the lioness to be contemplating suicide by

electric fence when the Great West Coast
   Earthquake of 2032 hits
and half of California drops into the Pacific Ocean.

I want a re-branded Casey Affleck bent on animal
   activism to use Ben's helicopter to air-lift the
   lioness from the rubble and bring her to Nigeria
where she will star in his big-picture Nollywood
   directorial debut about an ex-B-movie actor who
   finds his soul in the heart of a lioness,

making her the first Oscar-winning lioness ever,
transforming cinema overnight and relocating the
   centre of movie production from America to
   Nigeria (Hollywood being underwater).

I want the fame to go to her head.

I want her to become addicted to methamphetamines
   during a loveless marriage to the
   MGM lion
and blow all the money she made selling wedding
   photos to *Lion & Style* on promotional material
   for her all-Snoop Lion cover album that bombs
   after their messy divorce,

sending her to live broke and homeless in the
   Lagos metro system for a year where she finds a
   dog-eared trade paperback edition of *Pride and
   Prejudice* that inspires her to write a best-selling
memoir about her life experiences called *Pride Is*

My Nemesis,
penned entirely on discarded metro tickets.

I want Joseph Gordon-Levitt, Mayor of the World,
to get "Pride Is My Nemesis" tattooed around his
   bicep.

I want the lioness to have already gone off-the-grid
   by this point and have no clue when J.G.-L.
   breaks the Guinness World Record for "Longest
   French Kiss".
I want her to be settled in a zero-emission shack at
   the foot of Kilimanjaro, apprenticing as a basket-
   weaver.

I want to die in a horrible plane crash in remote
   East Africa.

HOW TO APPEAR PERFECTLY INDIFFERENT
WHILE CRYING ON THE INSIDE

Open the fridge.
Stare at near-empty jar of peanut butter.

Spread peanut butter on white bread.
Feel borrowed nostalgia for white bread.

Pour a glass of water.
Drink the water—does it taste weird?

Drink it anyway.

Walk around in the rain when it rains.
Open your arms to the air

like in the *Shawshank Redemption*
like you just don't care.

Break into the community pool
with your most attractive co-worker

and feel like you should kiss her
more than you actually want to kiss her.

Go to the library.
Log in to Facebook.
Scroll through newsfeed.
Scroll through newsfeed.

Hide in library bathroom.
Look out bathroom window

at the rain in the trees.

I CRASHED MY BIKE LAST NIGHT,
I WAS DRUNK

I threw the key to my ex-girlfriend's apartment into
    the Lachine Canal
and almost got hit by a train, because I was drunk.

I stood on the railway tracks after it went by,
and while gazing upon the lights of downtown,
    I yelled:

"What a bunch of phonies!"

I biked into Point St. Charles and didn't light a
    cigarette,
because I quit smoking, which suddenly seemed
    stupid,

so instead I bought a Snickers bar,
because I have to kill myself somehow.

I biked straight down Charlevoix, past dépanneur
    "Surplus Bread",
playing a game I like to call "Every Car Is Contem-
    plating a Drive-By".

I biked past a truck storage place and realized that
    there are truck storage places
and I tweeted:

"Put enough people in a place and eventually they
     will build too many trucks, and eventually they
     will build a place to store the trucks," and
     @stripmaller reply-tweeted,
"Entropy," and I reply-tweeted, "This is natural."

I helped Laura Broadbent pack up her apartment
     in PSC,
it's being demolished to make room for a fucking
     condo—

no seriously, fuck condos.

She gave me a bunch of her books and I said,
"I love you—no seriously. I love you."

I crashed my bike on the way home and fucked up
     my hand because I was drinking a bottle of
     white wine,
and the books threw off my balance.

I called my ex-girlfriend and told her,
"Someone said I looked like Ryan Gosling once."

She said, "It's three in the morning." I said,
"Some people say I look like the main guy from
     Bon Iver."

ON SLEEPING ALONE

Every night since she left it's the same:
the aliens turn on the tractor beam at 4 a.m.,

trying to pull me into hyperspace.

Then the whum-whumming fades away
and I am still alone in bed.

COMPUTER BRAIN VIRUS

Falling asleep last night, my brain caught a
    computer virus.

My mind's eye was the computer screen
and a low-res jpeg of the mall cop who caught me
    stealing oranges from Orange Julius when I was
    in 6th grade

filled the screen in a Windows '95 dialogue box.
I clicked the "X" at the top right of the screen—

but that was part of the virus.

The screen went blank except for the task bar,
the words "ORANGE JULIUS" where "START"
    should be.

The only option in the menu was "STEAL".

When I clicked it,
a low-res jpeg of the mall cop who caught me
    stealing oranges from Orange Julius when I was
    in 6th grade

filled the screen.

POISON DART FROG

When I woke up this morning
I was a Poison Dart Frog.

I was in a terrarium. I had a pond.
Across the pond from me

was a Chinese Water Dragon.
I killed it by hopping in its water dish.

My skin is poisonous.

My owner tried to pick me up.
I killed him too, hopped right inside his mouth.

I hopped in a cab, hopped on a plane,
flew back to the Amazon.

Had a Poison Dart Frog orgy.

Slept on the side of a tree.
When I woke up the next morning

I was a Poison Dart Frog.

THE KIM KARDASHIAN SEX TAPE IS
HARD TO FIND

The Kim Kardashian sex tape is hard to find
like a four-leafed clover.

Unlike the Paris Hilton sex tape,
which is the dandelion of my search history:

fair and mundane.

So I close my MacBook,
tack a glossy photo of Kim to the wall,

tear open a fucking clementine,
smash it into her face,

and whisper, "Take that,
you bitch.

You sexy bitch."

Then continue to read around
the Kim-shaped holes

in my *InTouch* magazine.

AT THE GROCERY STORE I FEEL
LIKE DYING

I am 100 depressed teenagers
at the grocery store

thinking *whatthefuckwhatthefuckwhatthefuck*

as a grocery store employee
places an avocado

at the tip
of an avocado pyramid.

MY ROOMMATES ARE DRUNK AND
HONKING LIKE GEESE

"A long, lonely walk,"
I answer to the question,

"What is sadness?"

in an interview
I conduct with myself

lying in bed,

in my salt-stained shoes,
on top of the duvet

at 10 p.m.

WORLD VEGAN DAY

"Throw the pumpkin off the balcony," I said.
"Baklava?" my roommate said, mishearing me.

"Pumpkin," I repeated, smiling,
envisioning the consequences:

What if the cops came?
What if the garbage collectors had to clean it up?

A stupid mess they didn't even make.

"Are you serious?" she asked.
"No," I replied,

"maybe later,"

then continued to read this article
about how octopuses are really smart.

LAST WEEK I WENT ON A DATE

In the courtyard adjacent city hall
there are squash that weigh

1000 pounds

and more. In the courtyard
adjacent city hall

they have erected
a ferris wheel.

"In San Francisco,

distances appear shorter
than they are

because of all the hills."

In the courtyard
adjacent the ferris wheel

there is a skating rink.

THIS WEEK I ATE ALONE AT A KOREAN RESTAURANT AND WATCHED PEOPLE ON A DATE

She flips her piece of kimchi over
like a TV chef searing a filet

between pauses in a conversation
about whether or not Tyler, The Creator is a
   "chill dude".

The third Hasidic family of the night
passes under the window.

Tonight is a holiday she can't pronounce.

"I think maybe," she says, biting her lip
to keep from crying.

He adjusts his ponytail

and continues to eat the big pieces,
like an uncle.

IN LINE AT ZELLER'S ON THE LAST DAY
ZELLER'S IS OPEN, EVER

I wait to pay for my discounted bottle
of Fructis 2-in-1 shampoo/conditioner.

A team of construction workers
swing sledgehammers at Zeller's Family
    Restaurant booths.

The woman ahead of me with shelving units
    in her cart
haggles the price of the floor tiles,

and I wonder:

am I attractive enough
to be in a shampoo commercial?

LOOKING SOUTH FROM THE WINDOW OF MY THIRD-FLOOR APARTMENT IN ST. HENRI AT 11 A.M.

- 3 large industrial buildings
- 40 cm of snow

- 1 black and gold Gucci
bathing suit bottom

- 1 fox-shaped cloud
swallowing 1 airplane

All of these things are true
I am a confessional poet.

HOME FOR CHRISTMAS 22 YEARS OLD

I eat Tofurkey
and watch Netflix

running my fingers
through my hair

like Pocahontas.

The Re/Max calendar
with the evergreen forest

and barn-red barn
tells me

it's Christmas.

100$ worth
of Chapter's cards

were given as gifts
this morning.

Now,

mom is in bed.
Dad is in bed.
My older sister
and her fiancée

are in bed.

My younger sister
plays Sims 3

on the computer
in the basement.

I eat Tofurkey.

I LEARNED HOW TO DANCE BY
WATCHING *SOUL TRAIN*

After jerking off to infomercials
for phone sex at 2 in the morning,

me and my BFF
would dance along to *Soul Train*

(not in a gay way).

Maybe a little bit in a gay way,
but mostly it was practice

for the Spring Fling Jr. High School Dance.

One time, a cologne commercial
between the infomercials

told us that cucumber-smell
is extremely arousing to women.

Before the Spring Fling Jr. High School Dance,

we rubbed cucumber slices all over our bodies
and grinded with like 5 girls each.

Thank you *Soul Train*.

GERRY'S DINER CALGARY, AB

I used to go to Gerry's Diner
when all the other diners had closed.

I met interesting people at Gerry's:
the drummer from The Riviera Heist

who taught me how to order
"coffee, black."

The waiters and waitresses,
who gave me no other choice.

Gerry's had a jukebox—
it was a 50s-themed place.

The first time I ate at Gerry's
I held Katelyn's hand

under the table.

The last time I ate at Gerry's
I was high on ecstasy

and needed somewhere to be.

Gerry's is a Hudson's now,
a franchise bar and restaurant,

and there is nowhere to eat past 3 a.m.
in downtown Calgary anymore.

IF I WERE FROM NEW ENGLAND THIS POEM WOULD FEATURE AN ENCOUNTER WITH A DEER

In Montreal I maneuver between
Gchat, iMessage, Facebook Chat, and Twitter,

all the while wishing that I was sitting quietly by a
    lake,
listening for loon calls.

I know I could drive to a lake if I really wanted to
but I just tweeted something clever,

and what if CultMTL wanted to contact me for an
    interview?

If I were from New England
this poem would feature an encounter with a deer,

but I'm not so I YouTube "loon calls"
and refresh my inbox.

SWIMMING LESSONS

Some people are swimmers,
and some people are pilots.

The bomber's hat I wear is brown.
High school was a long time ago.

Before she left me she said,

"Your flying dreams are boring and
why is your iTunes so organized?"

Here is a list of things I need:

- Seafoam paint
- Diving buddy

- A baby (someone else's)
to hold my finger in their fist

- Pair of flippers
- Oxygen tank

SAYING HELLO TO THE GIRL WHO CAN
WEAR HER HAIR LIKE A SCARF

"Bears that live by the ocean
will lift rocks in search of crabs

at low tide.

They looks ridiculous doing so,
like people in bear-suits,

and I will listen to any music
that sounds like it was fun

to make."

WHEN I WAS SMILING FOR 15 MINUTES STRAIGHT NOT ON PURPOSE

A dragonfly broke her wing
and I fixed it

with a piece of Scotch tape.

This required: the help of a friend,
a glass to contain the dragonfly,

and about 15 minutes
of concentration.

S-P-R-I-N-G!

Two flocks of pigeons bob above the rooftops
like a cheerleader's pom-poms, cheering

S-P-R-I-N-G!

"I feel like two Tamagotchi batteries
 have been lifted from my eyelids," Sarah says,

as a steamy laundry-scented draft rises
from the laundromat below

and two flocks of pigeons converge into one
to roost under the water tower.

THE STARS LATERALLY

I thought it was a big deal,
when I pointed out more than just Orion:

Cassiopeia, Cygnus, the Lyre.

She said,
"Have you ever thought about

the constellations between stars?

Project their depth into deep space
and view the stars laterally."

MONTHIVERSARY

I didn't bring you flowers
and I think it's because growing up,

I listened to N.W.A.

If I had listened to Coldplay while rolling around,
smoking weed, drinking 40s in a white Jeep,

I probably wouldn't have rolled around,
smoking weed, drinking 40s in a white Jeep.

I might have volunteered at the Y,
gone "Guerilla Gardening" like my mom suggested.

I might have brought you flowers
instead of this N.W.A. mix CD.

JFK POOL

The pool was blue
and bright and from a movie

set in 1961.

Sunbathers on the concrete,
tanned dads doing pike-dives;

a pregnant woman
in a vermilion bikini

looked absolutely radiant.

My book on Modernist French painting split in two,
so I put it back in my bag

and watched wisps of cloud drift by.

I didn't see a swan, or a chimera,
or Don Draper, or Cézanne's *Bathers*—

all I saw were clouds.

AT MOE'S ON DE MAISONNEUVE I SAT DOWN AND ATE A VEGGIE BURGER

On a Tuesday after midnight I came in from the rain
and sat down to order a veggie burger.

Only the cook, the waitress,
and my soapy plastic cup of water were there.

My burger had more mustard than usual,
which was wonderful.

A Beyoncé concert was playing at low volume
on the TV set across the booths from the bar

and she was killing it.

But what except four Ativan could I have swallowed?
to underwhelm the waitress who noticed my
    elated face,

because everything is wonderful
like more mustard than usual on a veggie burger
    at Moe's.

THE STRAIT OF GEORGIA, 5:30 A.M.

The sea kickflipped onto shore,
landed on my glasses,

and dragged them to the deep.

The deep is Blood Orange Mango Juice-coloured,
a reflection of the toxic sunrise,

into which I bat miniature nectarines
with a flat piece of driftwood.

I was supposed to meet my Japanese MDMA
dealer, Super Mario.

Super Mario didn't show,
which is why I'm the Babe Ruth of this shoreline

slugging as far as the eye can see,
which might not be very far—

I don't know, I don't have my glasses.

EVERYTHING TELESCOPES

Everything telescopes

when a jpeg of my mom
in a periwinkle raincoat,

on wet rocks the same grey
as her hair, the same grey

as the bottom of each cloud
over the beach in East Hants,

fills the screen like a star-chart.

MAGNETIC DAYS

"Sky" is a word that describes whatever is
    consistent above a person
from one horizon to the next.

On a similar note,

I keep seeing this girl Elissa who once borrowed
    my scientific calculator in 10th grade
in the faces of my new undergraduate classmates,

and everywhere I go people are smiling at their
    cell phones.

Today is better than the day I learned the *Ghost
    busters* theme on guitar—
even better than the day I first heard the concept
    for the Halloween costume "Edward 40oz.-hands".

I wouldn't be surprised if someone handed me a
    cocktail bun right now.

Yes, it's one of those days;

a day when I catch a beautiful girl opening her
    twelfth-floor window to lean out and smoke
    a cigarette,
and looking up at her looking down at the city, her
    forearms on the windowsill as if it were the

shoulder of God playing the latest version of
   "Earth" on PC,

I see her wonder why God put that Thai restaurant
   underground,
wonder what God's plans are for the abandoned
   post office,

see her marvel at the straight lines every person
   seems to walk in,
share her vow to jaywalk in parabolas whenever
   possible from this day forth.

The following thought isn't important, but I want
   to voice it anyway:

the amount of novels, death, and broken lease
   agreements
will only ever increase.

I bet not even Wikipedia knows what happened in
   1315.
I bet somebody used a clamshell as a spoon.

Sparrows are bathing in the concave tables on the
   patio at Second Cup after a sudden downpour
and the scope of my emotional project is
   panoramic as a song named after a freeway.

The sky will be pink tonight if the clouds hang
   around.

ON A DAY WHEN LAST NIGHT'S RAINSTORM HAS NOT YET LEFT YOUR BREAST

On a day when last night's rainstorm
has not yet left your breast

the Antarctica Foods semi-truck
is a chance mural of bell peppers and zucchini,

heralding auspicious encounters

like that between a child
and the five-dollar bill two sidewalk tiles ahead of her.

Entering the hardware store
to see if they carry the right size washer,

the sliding door chime harmonizes with the squeak
   in your shoe
and you realize that before music is music

it's just air in the room
vibrating at the speed of walls and light fixtures.

On a day when last night's rainstorm
has not yet left your breast

it's OK to sit in the park and eat a peach
wondering why Holden Caulfield is unaware of
   duck migration,

or if you pronounce "bagel" correctly,
or what your mom wore to the Sadie Hawkins Dance.

It's OK to leave your life's work half-finished.
Other people are writing novels elsewhere,

I promise.

No one is blowing their nose for anything less than
    an 8/10 necessity today.

On a day when last night's rainstorm
has not yet left your breast

there might be puddles from the rainstorm,
and if it is fall the puddles might freeze,

and if the puddles freeze you might crack their
    surfaces
with the precision of a Vulcan Nerve Pinch

in your rubber-booted toe;
if it is spring the puddles might accumulate

and the puddles might form rivulets
which might overflow the sewer drains, which is
    always fun to see.

If it is summer then it is summer.

Even the hair on your shoulders seem somewhat
    dignified.

There has been a great deal of consternation lately
regarding etiquette and the dog-earing of
    borrowed books—

I say go for it.

On a day when last night's rainstorm
has not yet left your breast

your text inbox is almost full—
deleting messages you know who is important
    and why,

and words like "suffused" and "Boeing 747"
illuminate your morning PB & J on pumpernickel

like a pinball machine bonus if you actually play
    pinball for a while
and get kinda good.

On a day when last night's rainstorm
has not yet left your breast

the air is an entity between you
and everything you might touch:

it is a womb.

At every moment you are about to be born,
perfect as a picture before it's taken.

FINDING THE MOON

Somewhere between ragweed
and the Fin du Monde bottles, a cricket is chirping.

I'm standing at what I call "The Great Junction",
where Mile End collapses into auto body shops

and entrepôts pour équipement de restaurants,
near Godspeed's first recording studio.

This is an in-between place.

A place a lot of Daves accept as a part of
    Who They Are,
like if scientists could extract their essence
    from DNA

it'd be baseboard heaters
and shale and rubber bands that snap when
    stretched.

A motorcyclist unzips the freeway.

The cricket shuts up for a second.

I can't see the moon but I bet it's awesome;

instead I have this elephant with a vacuum head
    for a trunk

(the logo for La Maison de l'Aspirateur)
which might be my favourite thing ever,
and a fire escape has appeared on my right—

I don't climb it. I'm not 16.

I haven't been 16 for a long time but I'm still
    doing this shit,
climbing fire escapes because I said I wouldn't,

finding the moon.

'If I Were from New England This Poem Would Feature an Encounter with a Deer' and 'Saying Hello to the Girl Who Can Wear Her Hair Like a Scarf' originally appeared online at joylandpoetry.com. 'When I Was Smiling for 15 Minutes Straight (Not on Purpose)' originally appeared in *Soliloquies Anthology* under a different title.